Table of Contents

I0448676

Page

CYBER

Critical Trends Converging

Several critical governmental, commercial, and societal changes are converging that will threaten a safe and secure online environment. In the past several years, many aspects of life have migrated to the Internet and digital networks. These include essential government functions, industry and commerce, health care, social communication, and personal information. The foreign threats discussed below pose growing risks to these functions as the public continues to increase its use of and trust in digital infrastructures and technologies.

Russia and China continue to hold views substantially divergent from the United States on the meaning and intent of international cyber security. These divergences center mostly on the nature of state sovereignty in the global information environment and states' rights to control the dissemination of content online, which have long forestalled major agreements. Despite these challenges, the United Nations Group of Governmental Experts concluded in a June 2013 report that international law and the UN Charter apply to cyberspace. This conclusion represents a substantive step forward in developing a legal framework and norms for cyber security.

Threat Environment

We assess that computer network *exploitation* and *disruption* activities such as denial-of-service attacks will continue. Further, we assess that the likelihood of a *destructive* attack that deletes information or renders systems inoperable will increase as malware and attack tradecraft proliferate. Many instances of major cyber attacks manifested themselves at home and abroad in 2013 as illustrated by the following examples.

- In March 2013, South Korea suffered a sizeable cyber attack against its commercial and media networks, damaging tens of thousands of computer workstations. The attack also disrupted online banking and automated teller machine services. Although likely unrelated to the 2012 network attack against Saudi Aramco, these attacks illustrate an alarming trend in mass data-deletion and system-damaging attacks.

- In early 2013, the US financial sector faced wide-scale network denial-of-service attacks that became increasingly difficult and costly to mitigate.

In response to these and similar developments, many countries are creating cyber defense institutions within their national security establishments. We estimate that several of these will likely be responsible for offensive cyber operations as well.

Russia presents a range of challenges to US cyber policy and network security. Russia seeks changes to the international system for Internet governance that would compromise US interests and values. Its Ministry of Defense (MOD) is establishing its own cyber command, according to senior MOD officials, which will seek to perform many of the functions similar to those of the US Cyber Command. Russian intelligence services continue to target US and allied personnel with access to sensitive computer network information. In 2013, a Canadian naval officer confessed to betraying information from shared top secret-level computer networks to Russian agents for five years.

China's cyber operations reflect its leadership's priorities of economic growth, domestic political stability, and military preparedness. Chinese leaders continue to pursue dual tracks of facilitating Internet access for economic development and commerce and policing online behaviors deemed threatening to social order and regime survival. Internationally, China also seeks to revise the multi-stakeholder model Internet governance while continuing its expansive worldwide program of network exploitation and intellectual property theft.

Iran and **North Korea** are unpredictable actors in the international arena. Their development of cyber espionage or attack capabilities might be used in an attempt to either provoke or destabilize the United States or its partners.

Terrorist organizations have expressed interest in developing offensive cyber capabilities. They continue to use cyberspace for propaganda and influence operations, financial activities, and personnel recruitment.

Cyber criminal organizations are as ubiquitous as they are problematic on digital networks. Motivated by profit rather than ideology, cyber criminals play a major role in the international development, modification, and proliferation of malicious software and illicit networks designed to steal data and money. They will continue to pose substantial threats to the trust and integrity of global financial institutions and personal financial transactions.

Other Potential Cyber Issues

Critical infrastructure, particularly the Industrial Control Systems (ICS) and Supervisory Control and Data Acquisition (SCADA) systems used in water management, oil and gas pipelines, electrical power distribution, and mass transit, provides an enticing target to malicious actors. Although newer architectures provide flexibility, functionality, and resilience, large segments of legacy architecture remain vulnerable to attack, which might cause significant economic or human impact.

Physical objects such as vehicles, industrial components, and home appliances, are increasingly being integrated into the information network and are becoming active participants in generating information. These "smart objects" will share information directly with Internet-enabled services, creating efficiencies in inventory supervision, service-life tracking, and maintenance management. This so-called "Internet of Things" will further transform the role of information technology in the global economy and create even further dependencies on it. The complexity and nature of these systems means that security and safety assurance are not guaranteed and that threat actors can easily cause security and/or safety problems in these systems.

2

The US health care sector, in particular, is rapidly becoming networked in ways never before imagined. As health care services become increasingly reliant on the cross-networking of personal data devices, medical devices, and hospital networks, cyber vulnerabilities might play unanticipated roles in patient outcomes.

Virtual currencies—most notably Bitcoin—are fast becoming a medium for criminal financial transfers through online payment companies. In May 2013, Costa Rica-registered Liberty Reserve—no longer in operation—processed $6 billion in suspect transactions and sought to evade enforcement action by moving funds into shell companies worldwide prior to being indicted by US authorities.

Emerging technologies, such as three-dimensional printing, have uncertain economic and social impacts and can revolutionize the manufacturing sector by drastically reducing the costs of research, development, and prototyping. Similarly, they might also revolutionize aspects of underground criminal activity.

COUNTERINTELLIGENCE

Threats posed by foreign intelligence entities through 2014 will continue to evolve in terms of scope and complexity. The capabilities and activities through which foreign entities—both state and nonstate actors—seek to obtain US national security information are new, more diverse, and more technically sophisticated.

Insider Threat/Unauthorized Disclosures

In addition to threats by foreign intelligence entities, insider threats will also pose a persistent challenge. Trusted insiders with the intent to do harm can exploit their access to compromise vast amounts of sensitive and classified information as part of a personal ideology or at the direction of a foreign government. The unauthorized disclosure of this information to state adversaries, nonstate activists, or other entities will continue to pose a critical threat.

Priority Foreign Intelligence Threats

Attempts to penetrate the US national decisionmaking apparatus, defense industrial base, and US research establishments will persist. We assess that the leading state intelligence threats to US interests in 2014 will continue to be Russia and China, based on their capabilities, intent, and broad operational scope. Sophisticated foreign intelligence entities will continue to employ human and cyber means to collect national security information. They seek data on advanced weapons systems and proprietary information from US companies and research institutions that deal with energy, finance, the media, defense, and dual-use technology.

TERRORISM

Terrorist threats emanate from a diverse array of terrorist actors, ranging from formal groups to homegrown violent extremists (HVEs) and ad hoc, foreign-based actors. The threat environment continues to transition to a more diverse array of actors, reinforcing the positive developments of previous years. The threat complex, sophisticated, and large-scale attacks from core al-Qa'ida against the US Homeland is significantly degraded. Instability in the Middle East and North Africa has accelerated the decentralization of the movement, which is increasingly influenced by local and regional issues. However, diffusion has led to the emergence of new power centers and an increase in threats by networks of like-minded extremists with allegiances to multiple groups. The potential of global events to instantaneously spark grievances around the world hinders advance warning, disruption, and attribution of plots.

Homeland Plotting

Homegrown Violent Extremists. US-based extremists will likely continue to pose the most frequent threat to the US Homeland. As the tragic attack in Boston in April 2013 indicates, insular HVEs who act alone or in small groups and mask the extent of their ideological radicalization can represent challenging and lethal threats.

Al-Qa'ida in the Arabian Peninsula. Operating from its safe haven in Yemen, al-Qa'ida in the Arabian Peninsula (AQAP) has attempted several times to attack the US Homeland. We judge that the group poses a significant threat and remains intent on targeting the United States and US interests overseas.

Core al-Qa'ida. Sustained counterterrorism (CT) pressure, key organizational setbacks, and the emergence of other power centers of the global violent extremist movement have put core al-Qa'ida on a downward trajectory since 2008. They have degraded the group's ability to carry out a catastrophic attack against the US Homeland and eroded its position as leader of the global violent extremist movement. It probably hopes for a resurgence following the drawdown of US troops in Afghanistan in 2014.

Terrorist Activities Overseas

Persistent Threats to US Interests Overseas. We face an enduring threat to US interests overseas. Most Sunni extremist groups will prioritize local and regional agendas, but US embassies, military facilities, and individuals will be at particular risk in parts of South Asia, the Middle East, and Africa.

Syria's Impact. Syria has become a significant location for independent or al-Qa'ida-aligned groups to recruit, train, and equip a growing number of extremists, some of whom might conduct external attacks. Hostilities between Sunni and Shia are also intensifying in Syria and spilling into neighboring countries, which is increasing the likelihood of a protracted conflict.

Iran and Hizballah are committed to defending the Asad regime and have provided support toward this end, including sending billions of dollars in military and economic aid, training pro-regime and Iraqi Shia militants, and deploying their own personnel into the country. Iran and Hizballah view the Asad regime as a key partner in the "axis of resistance" against Israel and are prepared to take major risks to preserve the regime as well as their critical transshipment routes.

Iran and Hizballah

Outside of the Syrian theater, Iran and Lebanese Hizballah continue to directly threaten the interests of US allies. Hizballah has increased its global terrorist activity in recent years to a level that we have not seen since the 1990s.

Counterterrorism Cooperation

As the terrorist threat is becoming more diffuse and harder to detect, cooperation with CT partners will take on even greater importance. The fluid environment in the Middle East and North Africa will likely further complicate already challenging circumstances as we partner with governments to stem the spread of terrorism.

WEAPONS OF MASS DESTRUCTION AND PROLIFERATION

Nation-state efforts to develop or acquire weapons of mass destruction (WMD) and their delivery systems constitute a major threat to the security of the United States, deployed troops, and allies. We are focused on the threat and destabilizing effects of nuclear proliferation, proliferation of chemical and biological warfare (CBW)-related materials, and development of WMD delivery systems. The time when only a few states had access to the most dangerous technologies is past. Biological and chemical materials and technologies, almost always dual use, move easily in the globalized economy, as do personnel with scientific expertise to design and use them. The latest discoveries in the life sciences also diffuse globally and rapidly.

Iran and North Korea Developing WMD-Applicable Capabilities

We continue to assess that **Iran's** overarching strategic goals of enhancing its security, prestige, and regional influence have led it to pursue capabilities to meet its civilian goals and give it the ability to build missile-deliverable nuclear weapons, if it chooses to do so. At the same time, Iran's perceived need for economic relief has led it to make concessions on its nuclear program through the 24 November 2013 Joint Plan of Action with the P5+1 countries and the European Union (EU). In this context, we judge that Iran is trying to balance conflicting objectives. It wants to improve its nuclear and missile capabilities while avoiding severe repercussions—such as a military strike or regime-threatening sanctions. We do not know if Iran will eventually decide to build nuclear weapons.

Tehran has made technical progress in a number of areas—including uranium enrichment, nuclear reactors, and ballistic missiles—from which it could draw if it decided to build missile-deliverable nuclear weapons. These technical advancements strengthen our assessment that Iran has the scientific, technical, and industrial capacity to eventually produce nuclear weapons. This makes the central issue its political will to do so.

Of particular note, Iran has made progress during the past year by installing additional centrifuges at the Fuel Enrichment Plant, developing advanced centrifuge designs, and stockpiling more low-enriched uranium hexafluoride (LEUF$_6$). These improvements have better positioned Iran to produce weapons-grade uranium (WGU) using its declared facilities and uranium stockpiles, if it chooses to do so. Despite this progress, we assess that Iran would not be able to divert safeguarded material and produce enough WGU for a weapon before such activity would be discovered. Iran has also continued to work toward starting up the IR-40 Heavy Water Research Reactor near Arak.

We judge that Iran would choose a ballistic missile as its preferred method of delivering nuclear weapons, if Iran ever builds these weapons. Iran's ballistic missiles are inherently capable of delivering WMD, and Iran already has the largest inventory of ballistic missiles in the Middle East. Iran's progress on space launch vehicles—along with its desire to deter the United States and its allies—provides Tehran with the means and motivation to develop longer-range missiles, including an intercontinental ballistic missile (ICBM).

We assess that if Iran fully implements the Joint Plan, it will temporarily halt the expansion of its enrichment program, eliminate its production and stockpile of 20-percent enriched uranium in a form suitable for further enrichment, and provide additional transparency into its existing and planned nuclear facilities. This transparency would provide earlier warning of a breakout using these facilities.

North Korea's nuclear weapons and missile programs pose a serious threat to the United States and to the security environment in East Asia, a region with some of the world's largest populations, militaries, and economies. North Korea's export of ballistic missiles and associated materials to several countries, including Iran and Syria, and its assistance to Syria's construction of a nuclear reactor, destroyed in 2007, illustrate the reach of its proliferation activities. Despite the reaffirmation of its commitment in the Second-Phase Actions for the Implementation of the September 2005 Joint Statement not to transfer nuclear materials, technology, or know-how, North Korea might again export nuclear technology.

In addition to conducting its third nuclear test on 12 February 2013, North Korea announced its intention to "adjust and alter" the uses of existing nuclear facilities, to include the uranium enrichment facility at Yongbyon, and restart its graphite moderated reactor that was shut down in 2007. We assess that North Korea has followed through on its announcement by expanding the size of its Yongbyon enrichment facility and restarting the reactor that was previously used for plutonium production. North Korea has publicly displayed its KN08 road-mobile ICBM twice. We assess that North Korea has already taken initial steps towards fielding this system, although it remains untested. North Korea is committed to developing long-range missile technology that is capable of posing a direct threat to the United States. Its efforts to produce and market ballistic missiles raise broader regional and global security concerns.

Because of deficiencies in their conventional military forces, North Korean leaders are focused on deterrence and defense. We have long assessed that, in Pyongyang's view, its nuclear capabilities are intended for deterrence, international prestige, and coercive diplomacy. We do not know Pyongyang's nuclear doctrine or employment concepts.

WMD Security in Syria

Syria acceded to the Chemical Weapons Convention (CWC) on 14 October 2013 and is in the preliminary phases of dismantling its offensive CW program. Previously, we had assessed that Syria had a highly active chemical warfare (CW) program and maintained a stockpile of sulfur mustard, sarin, VX, and a stockpile of munitions—including missiles, aerial bombs, and artillery rockets—that can be used to deliver CW agents. Until the CW materials are completely destroyed or removed from country, groups or individuals in Syria might gain access to CW-related materials. The United States and its allies are monitoring Syria's chemical weapons stockpile through the inspection and destruction process of the Organization for the Prohibition of Chemical Weapons (OPCW).

We judge that some elements of Syria's biological warfare (BW) program might have advanced beyond the research and development stage and might be capable of limited agent production, based on the duration of its longstanding program. To the best of our knowledge, Syria has not successfully weaponized biological agents in an effective delivery system, but it possesses conventional weapon systems that could be modified for biological-agent delivery.

COUNTERSPACE

Threats to US space services will increase during 2014 and beyond as potential adversaries pursue disruptive and destructive counterspace capabilities. Chinese and Russian military leaders understand the unique information advantages afforded by space systems and are developing capabilities to disrupt US use of space in a conflict. For example, Chinese military writings highlight the need to interfere with, damage, and destroy reconnaissance, navigation, and communication satellites. China has satellite jamming capabilities and is pursuing antisatellite systems. In 2007, China conducted a destructive antisatellite test against its own satellite. Russia's 2010 military doctrine emphasizes space defense as a vital component of its national defense. Russian leaders openly maintain that the Russian armed forces have antisatellite weapons and conduct antisatellite research. Russia has satellite jammers and is also pursuing antisatellite systems.

TRANSNATIONAL ORGANIZED CRIME

Transnational Organized Crime (TOC) is an abiding threat to US economic and national security. Criminals can play a significant role in weakening stability and undermining the rule of law in some emerging democracies and areas of strategic importance to the United States.

Drug trafficking will remain a major TOC threat to the United States. Mexican drug cartels are responsible for high levels of violence and corruption in Mexico. Drugs contribute to instability in Central America, erode stability in West and North Africa, and remain a significant source of revenue for the Taliban in Afghanistan.

- Synthetic drugs, notably new psychoactive substances (NPS), pose an emerging and rapidly growing global public health threat. NPS were first reported in the United States in 2008 and have emerged in 70 of 80 countries that report to the UN Office on Drugs and Crime. Although most global markets for drugs such as cocaine and heroin are stable or declining, the use and manufacture of synthetic drugs are rapidly rising.

The Department of State's 2013 Trafficking in Persons (TIP) Report notes that an estimated 27 million men, women, and children are trafficking victims. Virtually every country in the world is a source, transit point, and/or destination for individuals being trafficked.

Worldwide, money laundering totals more than a trillion dollars annually. Criminals' reliance on the US dollar exposes the US financial system to these illicit financial flows. Financial transfers and vehicles designed to obscure beneficial ownership, inadequate and uneven anti-money laundering enforcement and regulations, and new forms of digital financial services have the potential to undermine the international financial system.

Illicit trade in wildlife, timber, and marine resources constitutes an estimated $8-10 billion industry annually, endangers the environment, threatens rule of law and border security in fragile regions, and destabilizes communities that depend on wildlife for biodiversity and ecotourism.

ECONOMIC TRENDS

Global economic growth rates entered a marked slowdown with the global financial crisis that began in 2008. From 2008 to 2013, the global growth rate averaged less than 3.0 percent, well below its 30-year average of 3.6 percent. The lengthy global slowdown has meant lower job creation, income growth, and standards of living that many came to expect before 2008. Although worldwide economic growth will likely strengthen in 2014 to 3.7 percent, it will fall well short of its 2004-2007 peak when it averaged 5.1 percent.

Although emerging and developing economies will continue to grow faster than advanced economies, the gap between their respective growth rates will probably narrow to 3 percentage points in 2014, its lowest level since the cascade of emerging-market financial crises in the late 1990s and early 2000s. Combined with faster population growth in the emerging and developing economies, the pace at which per capita incomes in that group converges to those in developed countries is slowing considerably, potentially fueling resentment of Western leadership on global issues. Growth will probably be particularly slow among some of the emerging economies of Central and Eastern Europe, as well as Latin America and the Caribbean.

Stronger economic growth in certain advanced economies might mean a general tightening of global monetary conditions in 2014. Although such growth will benefit the global economy broadly, higher interest rates might pose new challenges to countries that rely heavily on global capital markets to service existing debt. Destabilizing outflows of international capital from emerging markets to advanced ones are possible in response to rising US interest rates and sustained recoveries in the United States and Europe. Tighter monetary conditions might also increase the risk of deflation in economies with slow growth, high unemployment, and low aggregate demand. Numerous European countries, in particular, have seen annual inflation rates fall below 1.0 percent and even intermittent periods of deflation. Such deflation might worsen the fragile finances of indebted households, corporations, and governments.

Declines in many commodity prices will probably continue through 2014. Although the moderation in prices is welcome from the perspective of major commodity importers, such as China, India, and Japan, and from the humanitarian perspective related to food security, it can pose balance-of-payments problems for commodity exporters, such as Brazil, Nigeria, Russia, South Africa, and Venezuela, especially those that depend on commodity export revenue to finance their governments. Forecasts in the past year project global trade volume to grow moderately in 2014 at roughly 5 percent; the World Trade Organization (WTO) notes that its growth projections are down from earlier in 2013, however.

NATURAL RESOURCES

Competition for and secure access to natural resources (e.g. food, water, and energy) are growing security threats. Rapidly increasing unconventional energy production and ample water and agricultural resources mitigate the impact of global scarcity on the United States. However, many countries important to the United States are vulnerable to natural-resource shocks that degrade economic development, frustrate attempts to democratize, raise the risk of regime-threatening instability, and aggravate regional tensions. Demographic trends, especially increasing global population and urbanization, will also aggravate the outlook for resources, putting intense pressure on food, water, and energy. Extreme weather will increasingly disrupt food and energy markets, exacerbating state weakness, forcing human migrations, and triggering riots, civil disobedience, and vandalism. Criminal or terrorist elements can exploit these weaknesses to conduct illicit activity, recruit, and train. Social disruptions are magnified in growing urban areas where information technology quickly transmits grievances to larger, often youthful and unemployed audiences. Relatively small events can generate significant effects across regions of the world.

Food

Increased global supplies of grain have pushed global food prices downward in recent months, easing the risk of a price spike in the coming year. However, natural food-supply disruptions, due to weather, disease, and government policies, will stress the global food system and exacerbate price volatility. Policy choices can include export bans, diversions of arable lands for other uses, and land leases to and acquisitions by foreigners. Lack of adequate food will be a destabilizing factor in countries important to US national security that do not have the financial or technical abilities to solve their internal food security problems. In other cases, important countries to US interests will experience food-related, social disruptions, but are capable of addressing them without political upheaval.

Although food-related, state-on-state conflict is unlikely in the next year, the risk of conflict between farmers and livestock owners—often in separate states—will increase as population growth, desertification, and crop expansion infringe on livestock grazing areas, especially in sub-Saharan Africa and Central Asia. Shrinking marine fisheries—for example, in the South China Sea—will continue to spark diplomatic disputes as fishermen are forced to travel farther from shore. Terrorists, militants, and international criminals can use local food insecurity to promote their own legitimacy and undermine government authority. Food and nutrition insecurity in weakly governed countries might also provide opportunities for insurgent groups to capitalize on poor conditions, exploit international food aid, and discredit governments for their inability to address basic needs.

Water

Risks to freshwater supplies—due to shortages, poor quality, floods, and climate change—are growing. These forces will hinder the ability of key countries to produce food and generate energy, potentially undermining global food markets and hobbling economic growth. As a result of demographic and economic development pressures, North Africa, the Middle East, and South Asia particularly will particularly face difficulty coping with water problems. Lack of adequate water is a destabilizing factor in developing countries that do not have the management mechanisms, financial resources, or technical ability to solve their internal water problems. Other states are further stressed by heavy dependence on river water controlled by upstream nations with unresolved water-sharing issues. Wealthier developing countries will probably face increasing water-related, social disruptions, although they are capable of addressing water problems without risk of state failure.

Historically, water tensions have led to more water-sharing agreements than to violent conflicts. However, where water-sharing agreements are ignored or when infrastructure development for electric power generation or agriculture is seen as a threat to water resources, states tend to exert leverage over their neighbors to preserve their water interests. This leverage has been applied in international forums and has included pressuring investors, nongovernmental organizations, and donor countries to support or halt water infrastructure projects. In addition, some local, nonstate terrorists or extremists will almost certainly target vulnerable water infrastructure in places to achieve their objectives and use water-related grievances as recruiting and fundraising tools.

Energy

Increasing US production of shale gas and tight oil in combination with ongoing energy efficiency gains will almost certainly provide the United States with a more secure energy future. Decreasing reliance on energy imports will reduce the economic impact on the United States of disruptions in global energy markets but will not insulate the United States from market forces. With a shrinking reliance on energy imports, an oil disruption will have a diminished impact on the US Gross Domestic Product (GDP), the current account deficit, and value of the dollar. The greater availability and lower price of natural gas and natural gas liquids will sustain the country's competitive edge in petrochemicals and energy-intensive production processes. However, some key energy-producing and consuming countries, which link US policy interests and energy imports, are concerned that greater US oil production will reduce US engagement in the Middle East and diminish US protection of critical oil supply routes.

Oil from deepwater deposits, tight oil, and oil sands will be the principal sources of new global oil supplies in 2014 and beyond. Oil extraction is trending toward production that is farther offshore in deeper waters, which might lead to increasing competition for desirable areas. Conventional oil production will continue to supply the majority of the world's oil, although discoveries are slowing and prospects for new sources are diminishing. However, conventional oil reservoirs also have the potential to supply significant increases in oil with the improvement of extraction methods. The exploitation of unconventional oil resources in the Western Hemisphere has the potential to reduce US, European, and Asian reliance on imports that pass through vulnerable choke points, such as the Straits of Hormuz and Malacca, or originate from less stable regions in the Middle East and Africa.

Extreme Weather Events

Empirical evidence alone—without reference to climate models—suggests that a general warming trend is probably affecting weather and ecosystems, exacerbating the impact on humans. This warmer atmosphere, wetter in some areas, drier in others, is consistent with increasing atmospheric concentrations of greenhouse gases. In recent years, local food, water, energy, health, and economic security have been episodically degraded worldwide by severe weather conditions. These include more frequent or intense floods, droughts, wildfires, tornadoes, cyclones, coastal high water, and heat waves. Rising temperatures, although greater in the Arctic, are not solely a high-latitude phenomenon. Scientific work in the past few years has shown that temperature anomalies during growing seasons and persistent droughts have hampered agricultural productivity and extended wildfire seasons. In addition, intense storms—including typhoons, hurricanes, tornadoes, cyclones, and derechos—when exposed to growing human infrastructure, contribute to greater damage and threaten ever-increasing urban populations and economic development. This trend will likely continue to place stress on first responders, nongovernment organizations, and militaries that are often called to provide humanitarian assistance.

The Arctic

Harsh weather and relatively low economic stakes have enabled the countries bordering the Arctic to cooperate in pursuit of their interests in the region. However, as polar ice recedes, economic and security concerns will increase competition over access to sea routes and natural resources. Some states see the Arctic as a strategic security issue that has the potential to give other countries an advantage in positioning in their military forces.

HEALTH RISKS

Health security threats arise unpredictably from at least five sources: the emergence and spread of new or reemerging microbes; the globalization of travel and the food supply; the rise of drug-resistant pathogens; the acceleration of biological science capabilities and the risk that these capabilities might cause inadvertent or intentional release of pathogens; and adversaries' acquisition, development, and use of weaponized agents. Infectious diseases, whether naturally caused, intentionally produced, or accidentally released, are still among the foremost health security threats. A more crowded and interconnected world is increasing the opportunities for human, animal, or zoonotic diseases to emerge and spread globally. Antibiotic drug resistance is an increasing threat to global health security. Seventy percent of known bacteria have now acquired resistance to at least one antibiotic, threatening a return to the pre-antibiotic era.

In addition to the growing threat from resistant bacteria, previously unknown pathogens in humans are emerging and spreading primarily from animals. Human and livestock population growth results in increased human and animal intermingling and hastens crossover of diseases from one population to the other. No one can predict which pathogen will be the next to spread to humans or when or where this will occur. However, humans remain vulnerable, especially when a pathogen with the potential to cause a pandemic emerges. For example, we judge that the H7N9 influenza in China that emerged from birds in early 2013 is not yet easily transmissible from person to person. However, it bears watching for its extreme severity, high death rates, and potential to mutate and become more transmissible. Between late March 2013, when the virus was first recognized, and the following May, when it was brought under control, H7N9 influenza killed over 20 percent of those infected and caused severe disease with long-term hospitalization in nearly all other cases. If H7N9 influenza or any other novel respiratory pathogen that kills or incapacitates more than 1 percent of its victims were to become easily transmissible, the outcome would be among the most disruptive events possible. Uncontrolled, such an outbreak would result in a global pandemic with suffering and death spreading globally in fewer than six months and would persist for approximately two years.

MASS ATROCITIES

The overall risk of mass atrocities worldwide will probably increase in 2014 and beyond. Trends driving this increase include more social mobilization, violent conflict, including communal violence, and other forms of instability that spill over borders and exacerbate ethnic and religious tensions; diminished or stagnant quality of governance; and widespread impunity for past abuses. Many countries at risk of mass atrocities will likely be open to influence to prevent or mitigate them. This is because they are dependent on Western assistance or multilateral missions in their countries, have the political will to prevent mass atrocities, or would be responsive to international scrutiny. Overall international will and capability to prevent or mitigate mass atrocities will likely diminish in 2014 and beyond, although support for human rights norms to prevent atrocities will almost certainly deepen among some non-government organizations. Much of the world will almost certainly turn to the United States for leadership to prevent and respond to mass atrocities.

REGIONAL THREATS

MIDDLE EAST AND NORTH AFRICA

Arab Spring

In the three years since the outbreak of the Arab Spring, a few states have made halting progress in their transitions away from authoritarian rule. Nevertheless, political uncertainty and violence will probably increase across the region in 2014 as the toppling of leaders and weakening of regimes have unleashed ethnic and sectarian rivalries that are propagating destabilizing violence.

- In Syria, the ongoing civil war will probably heighten regional and sectarian tensions. Syria has become a proxy battle between Iran and Lebanese Hizballah on one side and Sunni Arab states on the other. Fear of spillover has exacerbated sectarian tensions in Iraq and Lebanon and will add to the unrest. The influx of over two million Syrian refugees into neighboring countries will continue to impose hardships, particularly on Jordan and Lebanon.

- The turmoil associated with government transitions has prompted political backsliding in some cases, most notably Egypt, where the military ousted the democratically elected Muslim Brotherhood-dominated government in summer 2013.

- Public support for the governments that came to power across the region in 2011 is dissipating, a dynamic which will likely invite renewed unrest, increase the appeal of authoritarian or extremist solutions among Arab publics, and reduce the likelihood of the implementation of needed but unpopular economic reforms.

The following three regional trends will pose a challenge to US interests in the Middle East in 2014 and beyond.

- **Ungoverned Spaces.** The ongoing struggles for new governments in places like Tripoli and Cairo to extend their writ countrywide and worsening internal conflict in Syria have created opportunities for extremist groups to find ungoverned spaces from where they can try to destabilize new governments and prepare attacks against Western interests.

- **Economic Hardships.** Many states in the region are facing economic distress that will not likely be alleviated by current levels of Western aid. The failure of governments in the region to meet heightened popular expectations for economic improvement might prove destabilizing in vulnerable regimes.   Gulf States provide assistance only incrementally and are wary of new governments' foreign policies as well as their ability to effectively use outside funds.

- **Negative Views of the United States.** Some of the transitioning governments are more skeptical than before the Arab Spring about cooperating with the United States. They are concerned about protecting sovereignty and resisting foreign interference, which has the potential to hamper US counterterrorism and other efforts to engage transitioning governments. Additionally, the unhappiness of some Arab Gulf States with US policies on Iran, Syria, and Egypt might lead these countries to reduce cooperation with the United States on regional issues and act unilaterally in ways that run counter to US interests.

Egypt

The interim Egyptian Government has for the most part completed transition tasks on time, but Cairo's crackdown on dissent, including designating the Muslim Brotherhood (MB) as a terrorist group, has dampened prospects for stability and an inclusive government. Egypt faces a persistent threat of militant violence that is directed primarily at the state and exploits the interim government's lack of control over the Sinai Peninsula. Since 2011, the Sinai has emerged as a growing staging ground for militants—including terrorists—to plan, facilitate, and launch attacks. The level of protests and militant violence probably will not delay Egypt's progress toward legislative and presidential elections.

Syria

We assess that the Syrian regime and many insurgents believe that they can achieve a military victory in the ongoing conflict. However, given their respective capabilities and levels of external support, decisively altering the course of the conflict in the next six months will prove difficult for either side.

President Asad remains unwilling to negotiate himself out of power. Asad almost certainly intends to remain the ruler of Syria and plans to win a new seven-year term in presidential elections that might occur as early as mid-2014.

Humanitarian conditions in Syria in the next year will almost certainly continue to deteriorate. Ongoing fighting is driving internal displacement as well as flows of refugees into neighboring countries. The UN, as of January 2014, estimated that 9.3 million Syrians are in need of humanitarian assistance in the country—including 6.5 million internally displaced persons (IDPs)—and that at least 2.4 million Syrian registered refugees are in the region out of a July 2012 population estimate of 22.5 million. International aid agencies consistently face challenges accessing parts of Syria because of checkpoints, road closures, Syrian Government restrictions, and violence.

Iran

President Ruhani has heralded a shift in political momentum in Iran toward the center, but we do not know whether he heralds a reversal of the authoritarian trend in Iranian politics during the past many years. Iran's economy will continue to struggle without comprehensive sanctions relief, which drives Ruhani and his team of technocrats to pursue nuclear negotiations. Since his election, Ruhani has had the support of the Supreme Leader, which has silenced some conservative critics. Hardliners, however, have consistently argued that sanctions fatigue will eventually break the international sanctions coalition and are wary of Ruhani's engagement with the West, as well as his promises of social and political moderation. Ruhani must maintain the backing of the Supreme Leader in order to continue to advance his political agenda. (Information on Iran's nuclear weapons program and intentions can be found above in the section on WMD and Proliferation.)

Iran will continue to act assertively abroad in ways that run counter to US interests and worsen regional conflicts. Iranian officials almost certainly believe that their support has been instrumental in sustaining Asad's regime in Syria and will probably continue support during 2014 to bolster the regime. In the broader Middle East, Iran will continue to provide arms and other aid to Palestinian groups, Huthi rebels in Yemen, and Shia militants in Bahrain to expand Iranian influence and to counter perceived foreign threats. Tehran, which strives for a stable Shia-led, pro-Iran government in Baghdad, is concerned about the deteriorating security situation in Iraq. Tehran is probably struggling to find the balance between protecting Shia equities in Iraq and avoiding overt actions that would precipitate greater anti-Shia violence. In Afghanistan, Tehran will probably seek its own additional security agreements with Kabul, promote pro-Iranian candidates in the 2014 presidential election to increase its influence at the expense of the United States, and maintain its clandestine aid to Afghan insurgent groups. Iran sees rising sectarianism as a dangerous regional development, but we assess that Iran's perceived responsibility to protect and empower Shia communities will increasingly trump its desire to avoid sectarian violence. Hence, Iran's actions will likely do more to fuel rather than dampen increasing sectarianism.

Iraq

Iraq's trajectory in 2014 will depend heavily on how Baghdad confronts the rising challenge from al-Qa'ida in Iraq (AQI) and manages relations with the country's disenfranchised Sunni population. A pivotal event will be the national elections slated for 30 April. The Sunni population in particular must be convinced that the elections will be fair in order to keep them committed to the political process and help check Iraq's rising violence.

Iraq is experiencing an increase in the total number of attacks countrywide to levels not observed since the departure of US forces in 2011. Although overall level of violence remains far lower than in 2007, high-profile suicide and vehicle-borne improvised explosive device (VBIED) attacks initiated by al-Qa'ida in Iraq (AQI) in 2013 returned to 2007-2008 levels, roughly 68 to 80 per month.

The protracted civil war in Syria is destabilizing Iraq, hardening ethno-sectarian attitudes, and raising concerns about the spillover of violence. The Syrian conflict has also facilitated a greater two-way flow of Sunni extremists between Syria and Iraq that has contributed to AQI's increased level of high-profile attacks.

Yemen

We judge that Yemen has achieved provisional success in the early stages of its transition from the regime of Ali Abdallah Salih. However, it still faces threats to its stability from a resurging al-Qa'ida in the Arabian Peninsula (AQAP) and disputes over the future structure of the state. The government of Abd Rabbih Mansur al-Hadi has completed an inclusive National Dialogue (ND) Conference, but the parties have not reached an agreement on how to implement the federal state structure called for by the Dialogue.

- The Yemeni military's willingness to sustain pressure on AQAP will be critical to preventing its resurgence.

- Yemen's economy has stabilized since Hadi took office in 2012, but substantial foreign assistance will remain important to alleviate the country's serious economic and humanitarian problems.

Lebanon

Lebanon in 2014 probably will continue to experience sectarian violence among Lebanese and terrorist attacks by Sunni extremists and Hizballah, which are targeting each others' interests. The conflict in neighboring Syria is the primary driver of the sectarian unrest and terrorist attacks in Lebanon; already this year, sectarian fighting and political assassinations in Tripoli, Beirut, and Sidon have killed more than a hundred Lebanese. Increased frequency and lethality of violence in Lebanon could erupt into sustained and widespread fighting.

- Hizballah's secretary general, Hasan Nasrallah, has framed the conflict as an act of self-defense against Western-backed Sunni extremists who he claimed would target all Lebanese if the Asad regime fell.

- Sunni extremists have conducted multiple bombings in Beirut in 2013 and early 2014 in the Shia-dominated areas of southern Beirut that killed 75 and injured more than 500 people. Sunni extremists claimed responsibility for the suicide bombings in November 2013 against the Iranian Embassy in Beirut.

- Sunni Salafist leaders are calling for supporters to back the Syrian opposition, which threatens to escalate sectarian tensions.

Lebanon is facing increased challenges in coping with the continuing influx of numerous Syrian refugees. As of early January 2014, over 800,000 Syrian refuges were residing in Lebanon—roughly 25 percent of Lebanon's population prior to the Syrian conflict. Syrian refugees are straining Lebanon's fragile economy and burdening its weak healthcare and education systems. Refugees almost certainly will not return to Syria, given the continued violence and lack of economic prospects.

Libya

Nearly three years since the revolution that toppled Qadhafi, Libya's political, economic, and security landscape is fragmented and its institutions are weak, posing an ongoing threat to stability and cohesion of the Libyan state. Libya's democratically elected government struggles to address the many competing challenges that threaten to undermine the transition.

- Efforts by various regional, minority, and tribal groups to seek redress of grievances through violence and disruption of oil facilities are weakening national cohesion.

- Since the end of the revolution, federalist groups have declared autonomy for the east or south at least four times. The federalist-led takeover of eastern oil facilities in July 2013 has been the most sustained and aggressive pursuit of self-rule.

- Libya's numerous quasi-governmental militias often demonstrate little loyalty to Tripoli and challenge central government authority.

- The terrorist threat to Western and Libyan Government interests remains acute, especially in the east of the country, where attacks against government officials and facilities occur nearly daily. Regional terrorist organizations exploit Libya's porous borders and massive amounts of loose conventional weapons, further destabilizing the country and the Maghreb and Sahel region.

- To the benefit of the government, most Libyans oppose violence by federalists, militias, and extremists and generally support government efforts to usher in a successful democratic transition, including the drafting of a constitution and holding elections for Libya's first post-revolution permanent government.

Tunisia

Tunisia's long-suppressed societal cleavages and security and economic challenges will remain impediments to the country's political transition in 2014. The political environment since the ouster of President Ben Ali in 2011 has exposed sharp divisions over the role of religion in the state and the separation of powers. However, the Constituent Assembly's late January 2014 passage of a new constitution by a wide majority suggests an increased willingness among the parties to compromise.

SOUTH ASIA

Afghanistan

The status of the Bilateral Security Agreement (BSA) remains unresolved despite its endorsement by Afghan leaders during the mid-November 2013 Loya Jirga. Regardless of the status of the BSA, the bilateral relationship still might be strained if Afghan officials believe that US commitments to Afghanistan fall short of their expectations.

- The International Monetary Fund (IMF) estimated that Afghanistan's GDP growth rate fell from 12 percent in 2012 to 3.1 percent in 2013. It forecasts 4 to 6 percent growth in 2014 and beyond, largely because of reduced ISAF spending.

Afghan elections in 2014 will be an important step in Afghanistan's democratic development. President Karzai has stated that he will step down after the election; eleven candidates are currently competing to succeed him.

The Taliban, confident in its ability to outlast ISAF and committed to returning to power, will challenge government control over some of the Pashtun countryside, especially in the south and east. The Taliban senior leadership will maintain a structured and resilient leadership system. The Afghan National Security Forces (ANSF), however, will probably maintain control of most major cities as long as external financial support continues.

Pakistan

Prime Minister Nawaz Sharif's primary focus will be on improving the economy, including the energy sector, and countering security threats. Sharif probably won the May 2013 election primarily because the previous government failed to improve either the economy or the generation of electricity.

Islamabad secured an IMF program in September 2013. Pakistan satisfied IMF conditions for fiscal and energy reforms under its three-year, $6.7 billion Extended Fund Facility, paving the way for a second disbursement of $550 million in December. However, continued use of scarce foreign exchange reserves by the State Bank of Pakistan (SBP) to prop up the Pakistani rupee might make future disbursements difficult.

Sharif seeks to acquire a more central policymaking role for civilians in areas that the Army has traditionally dominated. His push for an increased role in foreign policy and national security will probably test his relationship with the new Chief of Army Staff (COAS), particularly if the Army believes that the civilian government's position impinges on Army interests. However, Sharif has publically stated that the Army and the civilian government are "on the same page."

Islamabad wants good relations with the United States, but cooperation with Washington will continue to be vulnerable to strains, particularly due to Pakistani sensitivities toward perceived violations of sovereignty.

- Prime Minister Sharif entered office seeking to establish good relations with the United States, especially in areas that support his primary domestic focus of improving the economy. Sharif and his advisers were pleased with his late October 2013 visit to Washington. Pakistan was eager to restart a "strategic dialogue" and its officials and press have touted results of the initial meetings of several of the five working groups that comprise the dialogue.

- Sharif also seeks rapprochement with New Delhi in part in anticipation of increased trade, which would be beneficial to Pakistan's economic growth. Sharif will probably move cautiously to improve relations, however, and India also will probably not take any bold steps, particularly not before the Indian elections in spring 2014.

India

In this election year in particular, coalition politics and institutional challenges will remain the primary drivers of India's economic and foreign policy decisionmaking. Any future government installed after the 2014 election will probably have a positive view of the United States, but future legislation or policy changes that are consistent with US interests is not assured.

- Coalition politics will almost certainly dominate Indian governance. Since the 1984 national elections, no party has won a clear majority in the lower house of Parliament. We judge that this trend will continue with the 2014 election, and the proliferation of political parties will further complicate political consensus building.

- In 2014, India will probably attain a 5 percent average annual growth rate, significantly less than the 8 percent growth that it achieved from 2005 to 2012 and that is needed to achieve its policy goals.

India shares US objectives for a stable and democratic Pakistan that can encourage trade and economic integration between South and Central Asia. We judge that India and Pakistan will seek modest progress in minimally controversial areas, such as trade, while probably deferring serious discussion on territorial disagreements and terrorism.

India will continue to cooperate with the United States on the future of Afghanistan following the drawdown of international forces. India also shares concerns about a resurgent Taliban in Afghanistan, seeing it as a long-term security threat and source of regional instability.

India and China have attempted to reduce long-standing border tensions through confidence-building measures, such as holding the first bilateral military exercise in five years in November 2013 and signing a Border Defense Cooperation Agreement during Prime Minister Singh's visit to China in October 2013. However, mutual suspicions will likely persist.

SUB-SAHARAN AFRICA

Sub-Saharan Africa will almost certainly see political and related security turmoil in 2014. The continent has become a hothouse for the emergence of extremist and rebel groups, which increasingly launch deadly asymmetric attacks, and which government forces often cannot effectively counter due to a lack of capability and sometimes will. Additionally, a youth bulge will grow with unfulfilled economic expectations and political frustrations; conflict will increase for land and water resources; and strengthening transnational criminal networks will disrupt political and economic stability.

The Sahel

Governments in Africa's Sahel region—particularly Chad, Niger, Mali, Mauritania—are at risk of terrorist attacks, primarily as retribution for these countries' support to the January 2013 French-led international military intervention in Mali. Additionally, this region faces pressure from growing youth populations and marginalized ethnic groups frustrated with a lack of government services, few employment opportunities, and poor living standards. Limited government capabilities, corruption, illicit economies, smuggling, and poor governance undercut development and the region's ability to absorb international assistance and improve stability and security, which would impede terrorists' freedom of movement.

Somalia

In Somalia, al-Shabaab is conducting asymmetric attacks against government facilities and Western targets in and around Mogadishu. The credibility and effectiveness of the young Somali government will be further threatened by persistent political infighting, weak leadership, ill-equipped government institutions, and pervasive technical, political, and administrative shortfalls.

East Africa

Security has increased and ongoing counterterrorism and policing partnerships with Western nations have strengthened in the wake of the September 2013 attack by al-Shabaab-affiliated extremists at the Westgate shopping mall in Nairobi, Kenya. Nevertheless, East African governments will have difficulty protecting the wide range of potential targets. Al-Shabaab-associated networks might be planning additional attacks in Kenya and throughout East Africa, including in Burundi, Djibouti, Ethiopia, and Uganda, to punish those countries that deployed troops to Somalia in support of its government.

Sudan and South Sudan

Sudan's President Bashir and the National Congress Party (NCP) will almost certainly confront a range of challenges, including public dissatisfaction over economic decline and insurgencies on Sudan's periphery. Sudanese economic conditions since South Sudan's independence in 2011 continue to deteriorate, including rising prices on staple goods, which fuel opposition to Bashir and the NCP. Khartoum will likely resort to heavy-handed tactics to prevent resulting protests from escalating and to contain domestic insurgencies. The conflicts in the Darfur region and in Southern Kordofan and Blue Nile states (the "Two Areas") will likely continue. Sudan will likely continue an offensive military campaign in the Two Areas that will lead to increased displacement and the continued denial of humanitarian access in the area. Darfur will likely remain unstable as militia forces and the government continue to skirmish, and as internal fighting among local armed groups, general banditry, and insecurity rise.

South Sudan will almost certainly continue to face ethnic conflict, resource constraints, and rampant corruption in 2014. Widespread clashes across South Sudan that began in late 2013 will make economic recovery difficult. Without a cessation of hostilities and a stable peace process, Juba will also struggle to rebound in 2014 because international partners will be more reluctant to invest after the emergency evacuation of foreign diplomats in December of 2013 and an increasingly precarious security environment across the country. Additionally, President Kiir will likely continue his authoritarian approach to running the country and dealing with opposition groups; any peace process will likely be slow and continue despite continued attacks by anti-government forces. Ethnic conflict in Jonglei will likely continue as the South Sudanese military faces internal divisions and threats from multiple rebel groups. We assess that Juba will continue to rely on assistance from the international community, but might lose donor funding following its heavy-handed approach to suppressing political opposition groups in late 2013 and it might be conditioned on any peace process. The oil fields, South Sudan's main source of revenue, might be threatened by anti-government forces, thereby decreasing or halting production. The South Sudanese government will also struggle to govern regions outside of the capital and provide basic public goods. South Sudan's economy suffered significant setbacks after Juba shut down oil production early in 2012.

Nigeria

Rising political tensions and violent internal conflict are likely in the leadup to Nigeria's 2015 election; protests and upheaval, especially in northern Nigeria, are likely in the event of President Goodluck Jonathan's re-election. Nigeria faces critical terrorism threats from Boko Haram and persistent extremism in the north, simmering ethno-religious conflict in communities in central Nigeria's "Middle Belt," and militants who are capable of remobilizing in the Niger Delta and attacking the oil industry. Unless Abuja adopts a comprehensive counterinsurgency strategy, military and security forces will be in a reactive security posture and have limited ability to anticipate and preempt threats. Southern Nigeria's economy, centered in Lagos, is among the fastest growing in the world but presents a sharp contrast to northern Nigeria, where stagnation and endemic poverty prevail amid insecurity and neglect. Given these domestic challenges, Nigeria's ability to project leadership across Africa and deploy peacekeepers will probably decrease from what it had in past years.

Central African Republic

Civilian casualties and humanitarian needs in the Central African Republic (CAR) have been severe since the overthrow of former President Bozize in early 2013 by rebel forces from the largely Muslim northeast. Communal conflict—largely along Muslim-Christian lines—has included formation of Christian militias, reprisal killings, atrocities, burning of homes, and destruction of religious sites across the country. The former rebels have used their de facto political authority to violently monopolize the country's most lucrative resources and territory, eroding CAR's historically peaceful Muslim-Christian relations. New interim President Samba Panza is a more unifying figure, but the government has almost no presence outside the capital and much of the country has devolved into lawlessness. In December 2013, the UN Security Council authorized an African Union peacekeeping force, supported by French forces, to restore security and public order and stabilize the country.

Democratic Republic of the Congo

Conflict in the eastern part of the Democratic Republic of the Congo has abated somewhat since the Rwandan-backed M23 rebels suffered a series of setbacks in 2013, gradually losing materiel support from Rwanda and control of its territorial strongholds. The conflict ended with M23's military defeat and the signing of an agreement with the DRC government in December 2013. We judge that M23 will probably not reconstitute and pose a significant threat to stability in Congo in 2014 without a substantial influx of troops and other military support from an external partner. However, Rwanda will probably consider supporting other armed groups in Congo to secure areas along the border, threatening attempts by the Congolese Government and UN forces to consolidate control of the territory. Other armed groups, such as the Allied Democratic Forces and the Democratic Forces for the Liberation of Rwanda, continue to pose significant risks to civilians and contribute to instability and violence.

Lord's Resistance Army

Pursuit operations of the African Union Regional Task Force in central Africa, enabled by US military assistance, has the Lord's Resistance Army (LRA) on the run and in survival mode, hindering LRA's recruiting and training. Increased cooperation between partners has facilitated information sharing and, combined with other efforts, enabled an increased operational tempo, leading to a significant number of defections. LRA still raids settlements in the Democratic Republic of the Congo and CAR and periodically abducts civilians. LRA leader Joseph Kony is often on the move and has long been able to elude capture. Getting a "fix" on his location will remain difficult in this very remote part of the world.

EAST ASIA

China

Chinese leaders will try to focus primarily on domestic priorities during 2014 while leveraging China's growing influence in the region. A new generation led by Xi Jinping is in place and its ambitious policy agenda is coming into focus: accelerate economic reforms, make governance more efficient and accountable, and tighten Communist Party discipline.

China will probably continue its increasingly proactive approach to maritime disputes, including a hardline stance toward Japan over the Senkaku Islands. More broadly, China's growing confidence, new capabilities, and other perceived challenges to China's interests or security will drive Beijing to pursue a more active foreign policy.

- Growing regional competition in territorial disputes and competing nationalist fervor increase the risk of escalation and constrain regional cooperation. Sovereignty concerns and resurgent historical resentments will generate friction and occasional incidents between claimants in the East and South China Seas and slow or stall bilateral or multilateral efforts to resolve the disputes.

Beijing has highlighted its pursuit of a "new type of major power relations" with Washington, but China is simultaneously working at least indirectly to counterbalance US influence. Within East Asia, Beijing seeks to fuel doubts about the sustainability of the US "rebalance" and Washington's willingness to support its allies and partners in the region.

China is pursuing a long-term comprehensive military modernization designed to enable its armed forces to achieve success on a 21st century battlefield. China's military investments favor capabilities designed to strengthen its nuclear deterrent and strategic strike options, counter foreign military intervention in a regional crisis, and provide limited, albeit growing, capability for power projection. During 2013, the People's Liberation Army (PLA) introduced advanced weapons into its inventory and reached milestones in the development of key systems. China's first domestically developed heavy transport plane, the Y-20, successfully conducted its initial test flight. Additionally, China has continued to develop multiple advanced ballistic and cruise missiles.

- Developments in PLA capabilities support an expansion of operations to secure Chinese interests beyond territorial issues. For example, China is pursuing more effective logistical support arrangements with countries in the Indian Ocean region.

- Elements from China's army, navy, air force, and strategic missile forces from multiple military regions participated in *Mission Action 2013* in September and October 2013. The exercise included two large-scale amphibious landings and coordinated long-range air force and naval air operations in a maritime environment.

North Korea

Two years after taking the helm of North Korea, Kim Jong Un has further solidified his position as unitary leader and final decision authority. He has solidified his control and enforced loyalty through personnel changes and purges. The most prominent was the ouster and execution of his uncle, Jang Song Thaek in December 2013. Kim has elevated the profile of the Workers' Party of Korea (WPK) through appointments of party operatives to key leadership positions and the convening of party conferences and plenums. Kim and the regime have publicly emphasized his focus on improving the country's troubled economy and the livelihood of the North Korean people while maintaining the tenets of a command economy. He has codified this approach via his dual-track policy of economic development and advancement of nuclear weapons. (Information on North Korea's nuclear weapons program and intentions can be found above in the section on WMD and Proliferation.)

RUSSIA AND EURASIA

Russia

Putin's 2012-2013 crackdown on the opposition defused the popular challenge to his hold on power; however, the Kremlin confronts a growing trend of opposition politicians taking their fight to the local ballot box. This trend was illustrated by the consolidation of support in Moscow around a single opposition leader—Aleksey Navalnyy—who finished second in Moscow's mayoral election in September 2013.

The Kremlin also faces a rise in ethno-religious tensions—as underscored by the October 2013 riot in the outskirts of Moscow—which will probably grow as the Muslim population in Russia increases. Moscow must balance an increasing immigrant Muslim population needed to offset its shrinking labor pool against growing nationalist sentiment among the ethnic Russian population.

In February 2014, Russia will host the Winter Olympics in the Black Sea resort of Sochi—an area bordering the turbulent North Caucasus region where Russian security forces have battled a local insurgency for the past 20 years. We have seen an increase in threat reporting just prior to the Olympics, which is not unusual for a major international event, and have offered assistance to the Russian Government.

Putin's claim to popular support and legitimacy as head of the Russian state has rested in part on a record of economic growth and the promise of stability, increasing prosperity, and relative personal freedom. The Organization for Economic Cooperation and Development (OECD) projects that the Russian economy will grow by 2.3 percent in 2014, putting at risk a number of ambitious Kremlin projects—including the $700 billion defense modernization plan, the 2018 World Cup, and social welfare enhancements pledged by Putin during his 2012 election campaign.

Moscow has hailed its CW initiative in Syria as a major foreign policy accomplishment. It positions Russia to play a major role in any future settlement of the Syrian conflict and adds legitimacy to the Syrian regime. Russia also will almost certainly continue to seek to fill the vacuum it believes is developing between the United States and Egypt.

The campaign to keep Ukraine from signing an Association Agreement (AA) with the European Union (EU) underscores the importance the Kremlin continues to attach to its goal of Eurasian integration. Russia will have to compete for influence with the EU in the West and increasingly with China in Central Asia; both will pose challenges to its pursuit of Eurasian integration.

The bilateral relationship with the United States will remain a priority for Russian foreign policy. We assess that Russia will continue its engagement with the United States on issues that address its priorities—Syrian CW as well as Afghanistan, Iran, and North Korea.

The Russian military remains a symbol of Russia's national power. Following measured improvements to its capabilities in the past year, it is setting its sights on the long-term challenges of professionalization and rearmament. The new leadership that assumed command of the military last November has made many tactical adjustments to the sweeping reforms the military enacted in 2008, but has largely kept the military on the same strategic trajectory.

The military in the past year has taken an increasingly prominent role in out-of-area operations, most notably in the eastern Mediterranean but also in Latin America, the Arctic, and other regions, a trend that will probably continue. Moscow is negotiating a series of agreements that would give it access to military infrastructure across the globe. These bases are generally intended to support "show the flag" and "presence" operations that do not reflect wartime missions or a significant power projection capability.

The Caucasus and Central Asia

Georgia's new political leaders have inherited pressing domestic and foreign policy problems amid high public expectations for progress. The economy, which has slowed since the Georgian Dream Coalition was elected in October 2012, will be an area of greatest immediate concern. The new government will also continue to balance a series of high-profile legal cases against former government officials for past abuses. The cases, while popular inside Georgia, have generated concerns of political retribution abroad and risk polarizing Georgian politics. Tensions with Russia have eased over the past year, decreasing the risk of renewed conflict. Progress nonetheless remains unlikely on the core disputes between Tbilisi and Moscow.

The standoff between **Armenia** and **Azerbaijan** over Nagorno-Karabakh and adjacent territories will remain a potential flashpoint. Neither side will see advantages in deliberately renewing hostilities, but prospects for peaceful resolution are also dim. Azerbaijan is willing to bide its time and wait for stronger economic growth to enable increased military spending to give it a decisive advantage. Armenia has a strong interest in maintaining the status quo because ethnic Armenians already control the separatist region of Nagorno-Karabakh and much of the surrounding territory. Nevertheless, the close proximity of opposing military forces and recurring ceasefire violations along the Line of Contact (LOC) continue to pose a risk of miscalculation.

Central Asia continues to host US supply lines that support operations in Afghanistan, and its leaders remain concerned about regional instability after the Coalition drawdown in 2014. Central Asian militants fighting in Afghanistan and Pakistan will likely continue to pose a threat, but sources of potential internal instability in Central Asia will probably remain more acute than external threats. Unclear political succession plans, endemic corruption, weak economies, ethnic tensions, and political repression are long-term sources of instability in Central Asia. Relations among the Central Asian states remain tense due to personal rivalries and disputes over water, borders, and energy. However, Central Asian leaders' focus on internal control reduces the risk of interstate conflict in the region.

Ukraine, Moldova, and Belarus

As **Ukraine** heads toward the presidential election scheduled to take place in 2015, political developments in Ukraine probably will continue to be shaped by opposition and public anger over the Yanukovych administration's abuse of power, the need for Yanukovych to maintain the loyalty of key elites, and his efforts to balance Ukraine's relationship with Russia and the West. Political developments in Ukraine will increasingly be shaped by public protests over Yanukovych's refusal to sign the Association Agreement (AA) and the presidential election scheduled to take place in 2015. Yanukovych backed away from signing the AA with the EU at the Eastern Partnership Summit in November 2013, probably because Moscow offered the only option for immediate financial support to avert a financial crisis that would threaten his reelection bid. Firmly intent on maintaining his hold on power, Yanukovych will probably resort to coercion, extralegal means, and other tactics to tilt the playing field in his favor and ensure his reelection, threatening a further erosion of democratic norms.

The first tranche of Russia's $15 billion aid package that Kyiv and Moscow signed in December will allow Kyiv to stave off a fiscal crisis in the short term but risks increasing Ukraine's economic dependence on Moscow. Russia's aid package removes incentives for Kyiv to enact painful economic reforms necessary to spur growth, and the ambiguous terms of the bailout leave Kyiv more vulnerable to Russian pressure, particularly on energy issues.

Moldova will continue to try to deepen its integration with the EU. Chisinau initialed an Association Agreement with the EU at the EU Eastern Partnership Summit in November 2013. It is working to formalize the AA, its associated free trade agreement, and an EU visa liberalization agreement before the scheduled November 2014 parliamentary election. However, both the EU and Moldova still need to sign the AA for it to come into full force. Moldova's pro-European coalition government suffers from low approval ratings after a series of political scandals and coalition infighting; its loss to the opposition Communist Party in the upcoming parliamentary election could delay or derail the country's EU integration course. A settlement of Moldova's conflict with its separatist region of Transnistria is highly unlikely during 2014 as they remain far apart on key issues and show no real willingness to compromise. Transnistria and its primary political and financial backer Russia oppose Moldova's EU integration; they also have little interest in resolving the ongoing conflict because that would remove a key obstacle to Moldova's European integration and risk reducing the influence Russia retains over Moldova.

In **Belarus**, the Lukashenko regime has managed to obtain the acquiescence of the Belarusian public, thanks largely to his regime's clampdown on civil society and also to Russian largesse which has enabled relatively stable standards of living. Lukashenko has done so despite a structurally flawed, centralized economy that leaves Minsk perpetually on the edge of economic crisis and in need of foreign financial assistance to stay afloat. Lukashenko's economic model has become increasingly unsustainable since his regime's crackdown on mass protests following the presidential election in December 2010. Continued repression of civil society has left him increasingly isolated from the West and with decreased leverage to resist Moscow's economic conditions.

LATIN AMERICA AND THE CARIBBEAN

Haiti

Stability in Haiti will remain fragile due to extreme poverty and weak governing institutions. Meaningful long-term reconstruction and development in Haiti will need to continue for many years. Haiti remains vulnerable to setbacks in its reconstruction and development goals due to the possibility of natural disasters. Food insecurity, although improving, also has the potential to be a destabilizing factor. Periods of political gridlock have resulted due to distrust between President Michel Martelly, in office since May 2011, and opponents in Parliament. Martelly is generally still popular, but politically organized protests, possibly violent, might occur before the elections, scheduled for 2014.

During the next decade, Haiti will remain highly dependent on assistance from the international community for security, in particular during elections. Donor fatigue among contributors to the UN Stabilization Mission in Haiti (MINUSTAH), however, will likely lead to reductions in force, evident by the 2013 mandate which calls for consolidating and downsizing forces. Although the Haitian National Police is making progress on its plans to increase force size from 10,000 in 2011 to 15,000 by 2016, the larger force will probably still need support from MINUSTAH to provide for its own security.

Central America

Central America's northern tier countries—El Salvador, Guatemala, and Honduras—will likely struggle to overcome the economic and security problems that plague the region. All three countries are facing debt crises and falling government revenues because of slow economic growth, widespread tax evasion, and large informal economies. Entrenched political, economic, and public-sector interests resist reforms. Domestic criminal gangs and transnational organized crime groups, as well as Central America's status as a major transit area for cocaine from source countries in South America, are fueling record levels of violence in the region. Regional governments have worked to improve citizen security but with little-to-moderate success.

- The gang truce in effect in El Salvador since March 2012 has reduced the homicide rate there, mostly among gang members. However, other crimes such as kidnappings, robberies, and extortion are undermining security for many citizens.

- Guatemala still has one of the world's highest murder rates despite lessened impunity for violent crimes during the past several years. Many areas of the country, particularly along the borders, are under the direct influence of drug traffickers.

- The homicide rate in Honduras remains the highest in the world. New Honduran President Juan Orlando Hernandez will likely prioritize security policy and seek to build a coalition within the divided legislature to push his economic reform agenda. However, weak governance, widespread corruption, and debt problems will limit prospects for a turnaround.

EUROPE

Key Partnerships

Ongoing US-EU Transatlantic Trade and Investment Partnership (TTIP) negotiations, European Parliament (EP) elections, the withdrawal of Allied forces from Afghanistan, and new leadership in the EU and NATO will create new dynamics in the transatlantic partnership in 2014.

- Europeans likely recognize the need to isolate the TTIP negotiations from the other issue areas. The TTIP has high potential for generating economic growth for both the United States and Europe and for reinforcing the transatlantic link. However, data privacy will probably become a political issue in the runup to the May 2014 EP elections; some opponents of TTIP might use the unauthorized disclosures of NSA information as political cover for their opposition to the TTIP.

- The NATO Summit in September 2014 will be an opportunity to reinforce NATO's purpose, as well as announce a new Secretary General.

Imbalances in the euro zone and slow economic growth in Europe are changing the political economy in Europe, potentially spurring support for nationalist and populist political parties.

- Radical nationalist and populist political parties are gaining ground in several western and central European countries and will probably do well in the May 2014 EP elections. In November 2013, two far-right parties—the Dutch Freedom Party and France's Front National—announced that they would cooperate in the EP elections and hope to form a new Euroskeptic bloc, probably linking up with similar parties in Central Europe. Public fears over immigration and Islam, alienation from EU policies, and perceptions that centrist parties are unable to deal with high unemployment and income inequalities will increase the resonance of the rhetoric of far-right and far-left radical parties.

Turkey

Turkey's foreign and security policy will be shaped by domestic events, especially the ongoing corruption scandal. Furthermore, the ruling Justice and Development Party (AKP), led by Prime Minister Erdogan, will be in election mode for municipal and presidential elections in 2014 and parliamentary elections in early 2015. The corruption allegations initiated in December 2013, allegedly by elements within the AKP associated with Muslim cleric Fetullah Gulen, represent the greatest challenge to Erdogan. Ankara will continue to pursue foreign policy objectives that maximize economic advantage for Turkey while proceeding with caution on issues that could alienate Turkey's nationalist voters. Erdogan's pursuit of a peace deal with the Turkish-Kurdish terrorist group Kurdistan People's Congress (KGK, formerly PKK) also risks antagonizing Turkish nationalists and neighboring governments. Erdogan is pursuing a multifaceted strategy of promoting domestic reforms and engaging the Kurds to end the armed KGK insurgency in Turkey. The protracted Syrian conflict is generating an increased extremist presence in Turkey, the primary transit country for foreign militants seeking to join the fight in Syria. It is also raising the potential for unsanctioned or opportunistic attacks by supporters of the Bashir al-Asad regime.

The Western Balkans

Despite many positive developments in the Western Balkans in 2013, the region in 2014 will continue to be characterized by deep ethnic and political divisions. The situation in Bosnia-Herzegovina (BiH) and ethnic cleavages in Macedonia are particularly volatile.

- In Bosnia-Herzegovina, different interpretations of the political framework, based on the 1995 Dayton Accords, as well as efforts by Bosniak, Croat, and Serb leaders to maintain control over their political and ethnic fiefdoms will continue to undermine BiH's central state institutions. Elections in 2014 will not likely bridge these differences, diminishing hopes for BiH's Euro-Atlantic integration that its neighbors have achieved.

- The Macedonian Government continues to push programs geared to promote ethnic Macedonian nationalism at the expense of the country's Euro-Atlantic integration. The longer that Macedonia's EU and NATO membership paths remain stalled over the country's constitutional name dispute with Greece and poor bilateral relations with Bulgaria, the greater the risk that ethnic tensions will increase.

www.ingramcontent.com/pod-product-compliance
Lightning Source LLC
Chambersburg PA
CBHW080802290526
45790CB00008B/3549